Arrows of Life

DAN M. KHANNA

Copyright © 2015 Dan M. Khanna

All rights reserved.

ISBN: 069238460X
ISBN-13: 978-0692384602

DEDICATION

To my precious gems, my beautiful granddaughters,

Jasmine and Jianna,

For their genuine love and hugs that brighten my life

CONTENTS

Prologue

The World in my Arms	1
The Touch	2
The Cracked Chalice	3
Two Lives	5
The Inner Voice	6
In Search of the Future	7
The Tormented Soul	9
Life is an Experiment	10
The Drinking Life	11
The Love of My Life	12
Dreams Die Hard	13
In Search of Death	14
The Drinkers	16
The Beautiful Life	17
Can I Love You	18
Can I Hold You	19
The Lonely Statesman	20
The Price of Freedom	21
Can I Live With You	22
The Wasted Year	23
The Wrong Love	24
The Wrong Destiny	25
The Misfit	26
The Loser's Game	27
The Illusion of Happiness	28
Destiny Denied	29
The Fatalist's Fate	30
The Luckless Luck	31
Killing the Dreams	32
The Lost Love	33
Time to Give Up	34
The Recluse	35
Searching in the Ruins	36

Accept the Consequences	37
Time to Move On	38
The Wasted Life	40
The Broken Man	41
Passing Life	42
Dashing the Dreams	43
Dare to Dream	44
The Broken Record	46
The Lonely Journey	47
The Relic	48
I am Wandering	49
Exit Gracefully	50
Love in Forbidden Places	51
The Greatest Loser	52
To Live With Oneself	53
Building Blocks of Life	54
Aiming for the Stars	55
Need to Depart	56
Series of Mysteries	57
Gathering the Pieces	58
Window of Opportunity	59
The Perfect End	60

PROLOGUE

One of the greatest miracles of life and its wondrous gift is the gift of life itself to observe the birth and blossoming of children, to me, especially my daughter and granddaughters, to see them grow with love, knowledge and wisdom.

They are the arrows that parents bring to their bows and point them towards the future and let them go. The arrows will land somewhere in the future, seed the earth and sprout it with new life that will blossom with myriads of colorful flowers making the earth beautiful, creating a new and better world for themselves.

> *You are the bows from which your children as living arrows are sent forth.*
>
> *The archer sees the mark upon the path of the infinite, and He bends it with His might that His arrows may go swift and far.*
>
> *Let your bending in the archer's hand be for gladness;*
>
> *For even as He loves the arrow that flies,*
>
> *So He loves also the bow that is stable.*

Kahlil Gibran
<u>The Prophet</u>

Dan Khanna

THE WORLD IN MY ARMS

When I hold you
I have the world
In my embrace
As if
What I wanted
In this life
Was with me
In me.
I am complete
Devoid of any desires
For all my desires
Fulfilled
Rest in my arms
Content and peaceful
Touching the soul
That unites us
Into a universe
Of our own
With all its beauty
Security and calmness
Mystery and love
Are with us
In our embrace
When I have you
In my arms

THE TOUCH

The gentle touch
Caressing
Tingling of fingers
Twining of fingers
Clasping of hands
Shudders a sensation
That vibrates
The entire body
Sending feelings
That arouse emotions
To hold you
To embrace you
Gently but firmly
Letting bodies touch
And explore each other
Seeking unity of emotions
Engulfing passions
To fire our bodies
Into an eternal fire
Of merging souls

It was just a beginning
It was just a touch
The touch

THE CRACKED CHALICE

I hold a chalice
With the elixir of life in it
That I want to drink
And be alive again
But I notice a crack
A gentle crack
That extends from the base
To the rim
I stare at it
To see if it will hold the elixir
Or, let it seep through the crack
I hold the chalice tenderly
Not trying to grasp
And break the chalice
For I like the chalice
It has beauty
It has curves
It has character
It proudly exhibits the crack
For the crack is part of it
It gives it dignity
A flawed beauty
That makes the chalice
A unique vessel
That holds elixir
Hope for people
As I lift it to my lips
The eternity passes
I savor the elixir
The crack has made it sweeter

I drink, I savor
I am alive
My love
The cracked chalice.

TWO LIVES

We live
Two lives
One for existence
One for our dreams
They are like
The two tracks of the train
Parallel, together and alone
Existing for a purpose
To hold a life
That travels on its shoulders
Towards unknown destination
Never merging
Never becoming one
The dream and reality
The two anchors of life.

THE INNER VOICE

The inner voice
That we must all heed
Is ignored by many
Stifled by most
For it is honest
It tells the truth
That we may not want to hear
For we want to hear
Only what we want to hear
Truth hurts
Ignore the voice
And continue with life
Creating follies
That just go on
Ignoring the voice
That eventually gives up

IN SEARCH OF THE FUTURE

There is a future
Ahead of me
I keep looking for it
I know it is out there
Waiting for me
But I can't find it
I take
Different paths
But I get lost
I don't give up trying
I keep walking
In all directions
Hoping to encounter it
But when I think
I am there
It vanishes
And I begin
My search again
This time
Determined to capture it
And hold on to it
But that is like
Holding air or water
Just a feeling
But not reality
It is there
But not there
It is where we go
But never reach

For it is a myth
That exists in our mind
As we continue
To search
For the future.

THE TORMENTED SOUL

Searching for solace
Travels through time
Trying to find a home
Where it can rest
And be at peace.
But, what about a soul
Restless and tormented
That disagrees with itself
Lives in contradictions
Trying to live in two life zones
It is neither here nor there
A home is
Where it rests
To continue its journey
A journey that crosses
Oceans and continents
Trying to find a connection
That merges itself with itself
It is a soul that searches for its soul
Within itself
Trying to extract some meaning
Into its existence
A lonely soul
A tormented soul.

LIFE IS AN EXPERIMENT

Life is an experiment
We are brought into it
But are not taught
How to live in it
We try, we blunder
We make mistakes
We score victories
It is an endless
Series of experiments
Some win, some lose
But, we keep trying
For we are part of life
And we have to live it
We are lonely
We are novice
That is life
We are thrown into it
And we must learn
It is an experiment.

THE DRINKING LIFE

The drinking life
Is a life of hope and despair
Hope for a future
That eludes you
Despair of the past
That abandoned you
You are alone
Drinking faith in a glass
That gives false hope
And bares truth at you about yourself
It is your friend
For friends and family
May abandon you
But it is always here
To give you solace
In the hour of need
But remember
It is short-term comfort
The illusion of pleasure
That numbs the pain
And for some time
We are at peace
In a world
That is uniquely ours
And then we wake up
To see the same old world
And pick up the pieces
Of life
That were shattered
By the drinking life.

THE LOVE OF MY LIFE

The love of my life
Is not with me
But she is always with me
In my heart
In my skin
In my soul
She is with me
When I am asleep
Holding me in her arms
As she rocks me into sweet slumber
She is with me
As I travel through life
Holding my hand
Guiding me towards my destiny
Gently swaying and prodding
She is with me
When I am down and sad
Gently holding me
Wiping my tears
With tender kisses
Consoling me
That she is there with me
No matter what happens
Whether we are together or apart
For love is eternal
The souls have merged
We are one
Forever.

DREAMS DIE HARD

There are dreams
And there are
Dreams of dreams
Dreams of a life
That one wants to live
A life that fulfills us
Our dreams are born
When we are young
We observe the world
And our innocent minds
Create visions
Of the world we want to live in
Simple and uncluttered
Peace and contentment
And happiness forever
But life is not like that
It plunders your soul
As it grinds you
The dreams become ashes
But in the ashes
There is still a spark
A smoldering spark
That is ready to ignite
And erupt into a bright flame
That lights the world
Telling the world
That I am alive
And ready to take on
Every challenge, every hindrance
For dreams are real
And I have
Dared to dream.

IN SEARCH OF DEATH

I know death is out there
Waiting for me
An eternal end
That engulfs us all
I sometimes wonder
Whether it searches for us
Or should I search for it?
I know that the end result will be the same
A quiet peace
But the process of searching
Can be exciting
If death searches for you
Then you elude it
Play games
Make it difficult for it
To find you
Just like hide and seek
That we played as kids
It was fun then
It is fun now
If you search for death
Then you taunt it
Stare at it
And tell it
I will be ready
Not when you want it
For it is a thrill
For why not die
On one's terms

It is a victory
In either scenario
We win, death loses
For even after death
We are at peace.

THE DRINKERS

The drinkers
Are a special breed of people
Who look at life
Through crystal images
And colored liquid
For it distorts the reality
And makes it into a dream
A dream that is real
As long as drinks are there
For why face the reality
The cruelty of life
When we can live
In one's utopian world
Of lies and deceits
But a reality in one's mind.

THE BEAUTIFUL LIFE

Life is beautiful
If you want it to be
Life is hell
If you want it to be
But what you make of life
Is up to you
Of course
The Divine touch
Does help
Life is a necessity
To get out of this world
So live it
Make it beautiful
For it may be
The last chance
As you fade into oblivion
With just a memory.

CAN I LOVE YOU

Love is real
It is a feeling
That I want to be
Consumed by you
So no one can extract
Me from you
Not even you
And that is the love I want
That is the love I feel
Can you handle it?
Can you live it?
So I do ask you
Can I love you?

CAN I HOLD YOU

My arms are empty
My body cold
Burning with heat
Trying to cool
But I need you
To hold me
Caress me
Touch me
Feel me
And give me a place
That is my home
Where I belong
Resting in peace
In your arms
Against your bosom
Sleeping gentle dreams
As I hold you.

THE LONELY STATESMAN

The lonely statesman
Is a noble soul
Trying to find some sense
In a distorted world
Straightening pieces
That are crooked and broken
As he struggles alone
In a world full of people
Yet very alone
To leave a mark
On an erasable life
To be forgotten
In the pages
Of a desolate history book
And such is the life
Of a lonely statesman.

THE PRICE OF FREEDOM

Freedom is a right
That we all have and must retain
And pay any price
Go keep it
For it is the only right
Worth defending
And paying with life
If it so demands
For no life is worth living
Without freedom
But freedom
Must be tempered with
Responsibility and dignity
Respect for other freedoms
And dignity of acceptance
Only then is freedom
Really a freedom.

CAN I LIVE WITH YOU

My heart cries
My body aches
My mind screams
Asking, wishing, imploring
Can I live with you?
So I can share every moment with you
With you around at every step of life
Every episode of life
Joy and sadness
'Til we blend into each other
To live a life
Of unison and harmony
Never apart from each other
Can I live with you?
Will you?

THE WASTED YEAR

As I reflect on my past year
I realize
That I wasted it
Did not do any worthwhile achievement
Lowered myself
To bare existence
Following the routine
Living daily to end the day
With no expectations
Life has taken over me
I cannot be at the mercy of life
Just passing days.

What a life!
Not the life I want
A life that cannot go on like this.

THE WRONG LOVE

The quest for love
Is a scary illusion
For love blinds us
And we fall for the wrong love
A love that is not good for us
It is there for the having
We embrace it
Not knowing that the pinions
Within it
Will prick us to death
But the pain becomes pleasure
For we are in love
And love must be good
And then dreams get shattered
We realize
We are in the bosom of hell
The wrong love.

THE WRONG DESTINY

I did start
On the right path
But somehow destiny derailed me
And I found myself
Chasing paths
That kept
Running away from me
And the wrong paths
Became my destiny
'Til I reached the end
And realized
That it is not where I wanted to be
But I was there
Alone and confused
I need to
Retrace my steps
And start again
So I can
Avoid the wrong destiny.

THE MISFIT

When I was born
I felt I was in the wrong world
At the wrong time
I was a misfit in life
For I had values
In a world
That had sold out to a system
A system of self-interests and mediocrity
A world that was becoming
Alien to me day by day
I stood alone desolate
Staring at the world
In which I did not belong
I truly was
A misfit.

THE LOSER'S GAME

The losers play
A unique game
That ensures
That they lose
It is okay
For as they lose
Someone wins
So in their losing
They win
But winning is not everything
Losing is learning about oneself
About life and its intricacies
It is just a game
Not to be taken seriously
For a game is a game
Just don't take it seriously
For no game is permanent.

THE ILLUSION OF HAPPINESS

Happiness is a quest
For most of us
Hoping to find it
In our lifetime
Yes, we do touch upon it
From time to time
We are occasionally
Glazed by its kindness
But for most of us
Happiness remains an illusion
That tempts us
But never satisfies us
We grasp it
But come up with empty air
We lunge at it
And hit a brick wall
As we settle into a routine
Of survival
Trying to make a living
In a greedy world
Struggling to meet ends
With dreams of riches
That may never come out our way
Hoping that riches will lead to happiness
Another illusion
That will soon burst
And we will keep
Staring at the wilderness
Hoping to carve monuments
With imagination and hope
As we struggle through life
With an illusion of happiness.

DESTINY DENIED

Destiny awaits us
Beyond the hill
It is there waiting for us
To embrace us
And tell us
We are there
But as I climb the hill
I see a vast emptiness
Nothing by eerie silence
As if I descended upon
A ghost town
From where all life is gone
I am alone
Wondering where my destiny is
It was there
Now it is gone.

THE FATALIST'S FATE

I am a fatalist
I believe
What will happen will happen
I may feel that I am in control
I am a puppet
That performs
At the whim
Of the puppet master
Laughing or crying
Awaiting my fate
With resignation
The fatalist
Accepts Fate
And resigns from life
With dignity.

THE LUCKLESS LUCK

We all want
Luck to be on our side
For it can guide us
Through tough times
And maybe give us breaks at times
When we need it the most
But, I await luck
I sit in its path
I move around
Hoping that it will find me
I wave at it
Yet it passes by me
Occasionally slaps me
To remind me
That I am not luck's favorite
I am luckless.

KILLING THE DREAMS

The dreams come and go
At night when I am asleep
During the day
When I wish what I want
My life to be
But dreams are dreams
Are they real?
Can I touch them?
Can I feel them?
Or, are they just an illusion
Of a life that I want to live
I had dreams
As a child
Dreams of an ideal world
Life and family
Home and happiness
The castle of cards
Came crumbling down
Lying in a pile
Disillusioned and disoriented
The dreams are scattered
Let it be
The illusion is over
Kill the dreams
And keep walking.

THE LOST LOVE

Love is never lost
But my love is lost
In the realities of existence
Love is pure
Untouched by the cruelties of survival
I believe in love
It is the only real thing
The only feeling
That binds God to us
The only feeling
That makes us human
If we can endure it
I quest for love
I try to find it
In any situation
Among humans
But the love I want
Remains an illusion
It is in my mind
But not in my life
I must still search it
For without love
Life is bare
And empty tree
That remains barren and dry
I must find it
For I believe in love
It is there somewhere
My lost love.

TIME TO GIVE UP

I tried my best
Maybe, it wasn't enough
But I am what I am
I am where I am
Yes, I could have done
Things differently
But I did not
I did what I felt was right
But right was not enough
For it turned out wrong
Right and wrong
Are two sides of the same coin
You never know
Which side will turn up
But as I played
With the dice of life
I counted on luck and fate
That abandoned me
To fend for myself
As the blows of life
Kept piling on me
Pummeling me
To the grind of dust
To remind me
That my time is over
I did what I could
But God was not on my side
It is over
It is time to give up.

THE RECLUSE

I am in a small hut
Isolated and alone in the wilderness
Shut out from the world
I have become a recluse
Creating my own world
That is free of prejudices and lies
Free of selfishness and exploitation
Free of greed and self-interests
Free of all the bad
That is in this world
A simple life
Where love and passion are sincere
It is okay
To be a recluse.

SEARCHING IN THE RUINS

There is a place
Among the ruins
Where my soul rests
After getting
Shattered by the storms of life
It is resting peacefully
Among its own kind
Abandoned and alone
Waiting for someone
To find it
And pluck it away
Into grand palaces
And illusions of happiness
'Til it gets shattered again
And cast away
To rest peacefully
Among the ruins.

ACCEPT THE CONSEQUENCES

I have no one to blame
For all the misadventures
In my life
Too bad it is an easy way out
But my life is my responsibility
Sure there are things
That I cannot control
But I am a product
Of my dreams and dilemmas
I am what I make myself
Good and bad
But in the end
It is my responsibility
I must assume and accept
The consequences.

TIME TO MOVE ON

I look at time
It is still swinging
It will keep on doing so
I ask myself
What is my time?
When did my time start?
At birth?
Or when I realized
That I am in a strange world?
I go through the motions
Just like a pendulum
Which never stops
But I am not a pendulum
Time for me will run out
It will stop
When is that time?
Though time never stops
It has stopped for me
Or, shall I stay it politely
It has passed me
I am left standing
Staring at it
As I wave to it
It does not wave back
Ignores me
For I am just one speck in sand

With no identity
I must rest
And stop the swinging

Just lay my head
On the pillow of God
And let time go away.

THE WASTED LIFE

As I gather
The remnants of my life
I reflect on a wasted life
Wasted on dreams
That crashed
As every wave smothered it
With the debris of ocean
Wasted on relationships
That sucked your heart
And left it like an empty shell
That longs for a song
That will never come
Wasted on friendships
That ended on a cul-de-sac
Trapped alone
With no one to guide you out
Wasted with relatives
That sucked every ounce of blood from you
In the name of love
Wasted with life
That throws me up and down
Like a ball on a trampoline
Enjoying the bounce
But having no home
Wasted with the world
That is corrupt
With the concepts of freedom and ideologies
In disregard of human dignity
This is wasted life
Not the life you want.

THE BROKEN MAN

I am a broken man
With the burdens of life
That I have carved
Since my birth
The scars on my back
Attest to the fact
But I am strong
My back is resilient
The wounds have made it strong
Now I can carry any burden
That life and world
Throws at me
They may have broken me
But not my spirit
For spirit has no back
It is wisdom
It is a Divine gift.

PASSING LIFE

As I stand at the zenith of my life
I see it passing by me
I gaze at it
Wondering if this life is mine
It looks familiar
I was on it once
Now I wave at it
As it pulls away from me
Hoping it will recognize me
And stop to let me get on it
But it ignores my gestures
And moves on
While I stand alone
With a raised hand.

DASHING THE DREAMS

The dreams that I had
As a young boy
Dreams of a future
Idealism of innocence
Creating a perfect world in the mind
A Utopian existence
Of a lovely home
Partner and family
A settled secure life
Great dreams, great expectations
But the dreams dashed
Like the waves
That dash against the rocks
Scattering and disillusioned
Dismayed and destroyed.

But dreams never die
Just like the waves
They keep on coming
Pounding relentlessly on the rocks
'Til it starts chipping it away
Slowly eroding the barriers
Then one wave
Lifts the rock
And hurls it away
Clearing the path for dreams
To advance and make a beached
On the shores of life
Dreams may dash
But they do not die
The power of dreams
Builds future.

DARE TO DREAM

I dared to dream
About the type of life
I should live
Knowing well
That the dream
Will just remain a dream.

I dared to dream
That I will be
With the love of my life
Living a peaceful contented life
But I am alone
That life remaining just a dream
That still makes me smile.

I dared to dream
That I will be successful
Living a life of respect and security
But now I struggle for a living
Trying to make ends meet
As I plan to work
'Til the day I die.

I dared to dream
That I will have friends
Of integrity and values
But what I got
Selfish materialistic friends
Where concept of friends
Was just to use and socialize.

I dared to dream
That knowledge and integrity
Were founding stones
Of a great society
But what I saw
A quest for mediocrity
Why think
When you can do without it.

But, I will
Dare to dream again
For I cannot give up
For giving up is accepting defeat.

THE BROKEN RECORD

My life is a broken record
Repeating mistakes
Messing up relationships
The pattern is consistent
Making money, losing money
I am good at repeating mistakes
Then I complain
That life is not fair
Like a record
That is stuck and repeats the same line
'Til someone nudges it
I need a push, a shove, a kick
Maybe then I will budge
Then stop complaining
That I am stuck like a broken record.

THE LONELY JOURNEY

Since the day I stepped into this world
It has been a lonely journey
Yes, occasionally I have met
Fellow travelers
Who gave me company
And then abandoned me
When their destinations came
A journey alone
Adjusting to life
With or without travelers
Each travel
Full of new adventures
Learning from experience
And continuing
To new destinations
Alone
But not alone.

THE RELIC

The relic
Is a person of life
That came and went
Leaving impressions
Of a forgotten past
That believed in love
To realize
That love was just grains of sand
That left you
When you held it tight
Relic of the past
That believed in integrity
Your word was your bond
Their word was a word
Faith and trust.

But now
The relic stands alone
Staring at the empty statues
Of faith and trust
The hollowness of integrity
As survival and selfishness
Lies and deceit
Make your innocence a crime
An ancient structure
To be admired and forgotten
An ancient person
In a modern world
Lost and forgotten
To be remembered
As a lost art
Presented in exhibitions
As a relic
To be admired from the distance.

I AM WANDERING

I started my life
On a straight path
And then I reached crossroads
Where I got lost
I didn't know
Which path to take
So I tried them all
And realized
That I was
Always on the wrong path
I just didn't belong there
I kept on changing paths
'Til I was on no path
I was just wandering
In the large landscape of life
'Til every direction was the same
I seem to wander
To endless mirages
And as hopes dashed
Each path become a burden
Endless search of life
That kept running away from me
But my quest is on
There has to be a path
Just made for me
Of rocks and flowers
It has to be there
As I wander
Still searching.

EXIT GRACEFULLY

The secret to a successful life
Is to exit gracefully
With dignity and self-respect
On your own terms
Not the terms
The world sets for you
It is your time
It is your precious moment
When you leave
The world of humans
For the kingdom of God
It is your shining moment
Time to shine like a bright star
In the dark sky
You are proud of what you have done
The best you can
You did it
Now, exit gracefully.

LOVE IN FORBIDDEN PLACES

Where does one search for love
Among the faces of humanity
Or in forbidden places?
For treasures are found
In dark dungeons
The bright humanity
Projects a facade of lights
That blinds you
While darkness lurches behind
In the deadly depths
Hide a growing life
That can blossom
And hurl you into space
To search for love
That's where you will find
True love.

THE GREATEST LOSER

The greatest loser
Stands in front of the Almighty
And roars
You made me a loser
I was born
To shape humankind
But instead
I could not even shape my life
Everything I touched disintegrated
Everything I dreamed disappeared
Everything I built
I destroyed
Why me?
Do I have to go out
As the greatest loser in the world?
Why do I get this honor?
What have I done to deserve this?
I tried
I made an effort
But when I die
I will be alone
Forgotten
Like most people on earth
But I did try
Nothing worked
Now I stand in front of You
And demand an answer
Why me?

TO LIVE WITH ONESELF

There is nothing harder
Than trying to live with oneself
For oneself is true
It tells the truth
It is honest
It is objective
It has no hidden agenda
It is your best friend
But we ignore it
For we are afraid of truth
It may tell us
What we don't want to hear
We are scared of it
For to be with oneself is pure
But we live in a contaminated world
So we ignore the truth
For an artificial world
For living with oneself
Is not easy.

BUILDING BLOCKS OF LIFE

Life is made of blocks
That we put together
To create a structure of our liking
Some tall, some big
Some small, some narrow
Blocks stacked on each other
Precociously and gently
Always vulnerable to unknown forces
That can disintegrate its structure
But the blocks rest on harmony
Not knowing when they will tumble
The building blocks of life.

AIMING FOR THE STARS

We aim for the stars
Not knowing what that star is
Where that star is
But it feels good
For it is up there
Just like our dreams
But the star is distant
It is near, yet so far
You can see it
But not touch it
It is bright
Just like your ambition
But it is just
One of many stars
Which one is mine?
I don't know
Will I reach it?
I don't know
But I still
Aim for the star.

NEED TO DEPART

The train has come and gone
I remain stranded on the station
Waiting for that one final train
That will finally take me
On my last journey
To a place where I want to rest in peace
A place I can call my home
My bags are packed
All my life's possessions
In a battered trunk
The only thing that has lived with me
Holding all I own
To remind me that all my life
Can be placed in this trunk
It is all I had
It is all I have
True life's possessions are few
Simple memories of a normal existence
As we accumulate material possessions
We don't realize how little we really need
My trunk is my existence
The train comes
My destination's name is on it
I board with my trunk
The train moves
As landscapes skip by me
I realize I am heading home
All I want is with me
Time to start a new life.

SERIES OF MYSTERIES

All lives are series of mysteries
Why are we born?
Why to our parents?
Why in this part of the world?
Our entire life then is challenged
To unravel the mysteries
Some are easy to solve
Some difficult
But as we try to solve our mysteries
We discover ourselves
And are amazed by what we see
We didn't know us
But now we stand
Hand in hand with ourselves
Happy that we have solved the mystery
An illusion of my story
That goes on.

GATHERING THE PIECES

The shattered glass
Spread across the marble floor
Some large, some small
Some you can't even see
But deadly
I kneel to gather the pieces
Sweep into a container
So as not to hurt anyone
Gently but thoroughly
But do I know I got all the pieces
I never will
As I step on the floor
I wonder did I miss a piece
Will I step on it?
Will I bleed?
Did I get all?
I will never know.

WINDOW OF OPPORTUNITY

There is a small window
That remains shut most of the time
It is the window to watch
For it has the best view
It has fresh breeze
But we ignore it most of the time

For it is too small
The big windows offer great views
Of known scenes
The breeze is familiar
Easy to open
But it is the small window
That remains shut and stuck
For it opens doors to a world
A future that is ours
It is the window of opportunity
The only window that matters.

THE PERFECT END

Robert Browning wrote:
"Grow old along with me
the best is yet to be
the last of life
for which, the first was made."

Is the last of life the best?
What is a perfect end to an imperfect life?
Passing away peacefully while soundly asleep
Surrounded by your loved ones
A ceremonial funeral
A glowing obituary
Attendance of dignitaries
A praising eulogy
Do not speak evil of the dead
But to the dead
It does not matter
What matters is that you die
On your own terms
Quietly alone
So no one has much to say
That is a perfect end.

ABOUT THE AUTHOR

Dan Khanna considers himself a traveler through life enjoying an adventurous journey. Dan was born in New Delhi, India. After he completed high school, at St. Columbus High School, Dan left India striking out for California via short stays in London, Montreal and Milwaukee, Wisconsin. Although his dream was to pursue a career in the arts, acting, music, and writing, a quirk of fate placed him in engineering college and pursuing a business management career, in which he excelled. Dan completed an undergraduate program in engineering, and a Master and Doctorate in Business Administration.

Dan worked in Silicon Valley's high technology firms and was a CEO and founder of several firms. He changed careers to be a professor. Now, he again is pursuing his dream in creative endeavors.

Dan is the quintessential Renaissance Man, whose interests span the gamut of the arts, sciences, history, social and political studies, classics and philosophy. His search for knowledge began in his early life where his father was the Chief Education Officer of Delhi and his mother was a Sanskrit scholar. Dan speaks English, Hindi, Urdu, Punjabi, and Gujarati.

As a child, Dan read voraciously, particularly enjoying novels, such as Sherlock Holmes, Agatha Christie, Earl Stanley Gardener, Ian Fleming's James Bond series and classic works of Shakespeare, Tolstoy, Dickens, Oscar Wilde, Thomas Hardy, and other writers. He was very interested in poetry and read English poems of Browning, Keats, Milton, Tennyson, and Frost, as well as, other poets, while mastering Urdu poetry. His intellectual interests including studying Western and Eastern philosophers, especially Socrates, from whom he learned questioning methodology employed in his research, lectures and seminars.

During his parochial education, Dan was interested in various sports: cricket, soccer and field hockey. His love for the arts and music was honed to a level that he performed in plays, movies and solo concerts.

Dan's present journey is devoted to creative arts and activities, primarily writing poetry, fiction and non-fiction books and plays, while continuing to acquire knowledge of diverse subjects. He has published one book and has written over twelve hundred poems. Dan has several non-fiction and fiction books in development.

www.ingramcontent.com/pod-product-compliance
Lightning Source LLC
Chambersburg PA
CBHW071415040426
42444CB00009B/2263